The Renaissance

Contents

An Uncomfortable Visit In 1508, Desiderius Erasmus (des uh DAIR ee us ih RAZ mus), the greatest European scholar of his age, journeyed from Holland to Venice, Italy. There, he stayed in the home of the foremost printer in Italy—Aldus Manutius (AWL dus muh NOO shee us).

Erasmus found his lodgings most uncomfortable. The printer's house was drafty in winter and so full of fleas and bed bugs in summer that Erasmus could hardly sleep. As many as 30 scholars stayed in the printer's home at any one time. Manutius had little money to spend to make his guests comfortable. He provided the cook with moldy flour for baking and served up a meal of thin soup, hard cheese, and tough beef.

Why would Erasmus and other scholars travel long distances to Italy and endure uncomfortable living conditions? These scholars all shared an intense desire to learn more about the civilizations of ancient Greece and Rome. They were fascinated with works of classical literature, including the philosophical works of Plato (PLAYT oh), the poems of Virgil, and the orations of Cicero (SIHS ur oh). All around Italy these works were being rediscovered and studied.

At the printer's dinner table, the scholars talked about Plato and Cicero, exchanged ideas concerning ancient civilizations, described their projects and dreams, and commented on one another's work. What's more, they did all of these things in ancient Greek! If anyone slipped into another language, he was fined.

The scholars were dissatisfied with the world in which they had grown up. They felt that they had been born in an uncultured age in which people had forgotten about the great writers of Greece and Rome. They grumbled that the last several centuries had been centuries of famine, plague, warfare, ignorance, and superstition. Unfairly, some of them even dismissed the previous 1,000 years as the Dark Ages.

This dissatisfaction with the recent past made these men so excited about what was happening in Italy in their own day. In Italy the wisdom of the ancient Greeks and Romans was being rediscovered. Scholars known as humanists had been rummaging around in monasteries and cathedral libraries, digging up copies of ancient Greek and Roman books that had long been neglected. They were called "humanists" because of the subjects we call the humanities, including history, languages, and literature.

Erasmus saw that the rediscovery of ancient Greek and Roman written works opened fresh areas of thought.

These manuscripts covered a wide range of topics. Some treated philosophy or history. Others had to do with literature, grammar, or

rhetoric. Still others had to do with art and architecture. The humanists studied the manuscripts they recovered with loving care. They compared and corrected them, translated and explained them. In the days before printing was invented, they made copies of their manuscripts by hand. After printing was invented, they began to give their precious manuscripts to a printer like Erasmus's host to publish.

When Erasmus contemplated the humanist movement of which he was a part, he felt he was witnessing the dawning of a brighter day. The other scholars around the dinner table were equally enthusiastic. They felt that they were participating in a rediscovery of the ancient civilizations of Greece and Rome, a rebirth of culture, literature, and the arts.

What All the Excitement Was About

What Erasmus and his fellow scholars were so excited about was the energetic period of change that we now call the Renaissance. *Renaissance* is the French word for "rebirth." When we speak of the Renaissance, we are referring to a period in history when a rediscovery of classical learning led to great achievements, not only in literature but also in philosophy, education, architecture, sculpture, and painting.

The Renaissance began in Italy about the middle of the fourteenth century, when scholars began uncovering and studying forgotten manuscripts in Greek and Latin. For the next 200 or so years (1350–1550), the center of creative and scholarly activity moved from one major Italian city-state to another, with Florence, Rome, and Venice all playing major roles. Later, in the sixteenth and seventeenth centuries, the spirit of the Renaissance spread to other places in Europe, including Germany, France, Spain, and England.

Although the Renaissance began with the rediscovery of old manuscripts, it didn't end there. The humanists dug up manuscripts on art, architecture, and literature, and these manuscripts led to increased interest in all these fields. Soon, people were digging up Greek and Roman statues and marveling at their beauty. Renaissance sculptors worked hard to capture the same beauty in their own creations. Painters were also inspired by Greek and Roman art; as the years went by, more and more of them modeled their works on Greek and Roman examples rather than on the more recent work of medieval artists. Architects studied ancient buildings and used them as models for new buildings. Renaissance poets tried to write poems as great (they thought) as the ancient poets had written. All these artists were using old art to create new art.

Once people saw what marvelous things human beings could create, they began to develop a new appreciation of humanity. Renaissance artists did not forget about God, but they started drawing more attention in their art to human beings. The paintings and sculptures they made had many different subjects. Some were about religion, and others portrayed historical events or tales from Greek and Roman literature and myths. They also made portraits. Since the Bible told them that people were created in the image of God, they believed that our creative powers are a gift from God and deserve special attention.

The Italian humanist Pico della Mirandola (PEE koh DAYL lah mee RAHN doh lah) captured this new feeling when he wrote his *Oration on the Dignity of Man*. In it, Pico argues that "there is nothing . . . more wonderful than man." According to Pico, man is "a miracle," for human beings are "constrained [held back] by no limits" and are able to become whatever they wish to become.

Important Renaissance Figures

Many years later the greatest writer of the English Renaissance, William Shakespeare, had one of his most famous dramatic characters hold forth on the same theme: "What a piece of work is a man!" exclaims Prince Hamlet. "How noble in reason! how infinite in faculty! in form and moving how express and admirable! in action how like an angel! in apprehension [understanding] how like a god! the beauty of the world! the paragon [greatest] of animals!" You don't need to understand every word that Hamlet says to feel the excitement in his voice and understand that, in these lines, he is thinking like a Renaissance humanist.

Shakespeare, Pico, and Erasmus are only three of many Renaissance figures who are still widely admired today. Others include the Italian artists Raphael (rah fah EL), Leonardo da Vinci (duh VIHN chee), and Michelangelo (mye kul AN juh loh); the Italian political writer Machiavelli (mak ee uh VEL ee); and the great Spanish novelist Cervantes (sur VAN teez). Indeed, perhaps no age in history has produced more eminent artists and writers than the Renaissance. In this unit you will learn about some of the most important of these artists and writers. But before we turn to individuals, let's look at some reasons why the Renaissance began where it did.

Italy the Innovator

As you read the opening paragraphs of this lesson, you may have been wondering why the Renaissance began in Italy and not in England or Germany. Scholars have argued about that question for years and have suggested some reasons why Italy led the way.

For one thing, Italy had been the center of the ancient Roman Empire. The ruins of that great empire surrounded the inhabitants of Italy: crumbling walls and toppled columns, arenas and temples overrun with weeds, once-splendid roads long ago fallen into disrepair. These reminders ensured that Ancient Rome was never entirely forgotten.

Business and commerce also helped pave the way for the Italian Renaissance. Italy is a boot-shaped peninsula, jutting out into the Mediterranean Sea. Trading ships sailed back and forth across the Mediterranean, from western Europe to the Middle East and from northern Africa to southern Europe. Because of its central location, Italy was in a good position to profit from this trade.

During the Renaissance there was no central government in Italy. Instead, the peninsula was divided into more than 250 city-states—most of them tiny, but some larger, like Florence, Venice, Milan, and Genoa. A city-state is like a small country. At its heart is a city that is the center of government and business, but it also includes the countryside with its farms and villages. Many of these city-states were located on the sea, or on rivers near the sea, and they used their advantageous locations to gain wealth by trading with

You can see how the ruins of the Forum, a public meeting place in Ancient Rome, influenced late Renaissance buildings such as the church in the background of this photograph.

4

Italy During the Renaissance

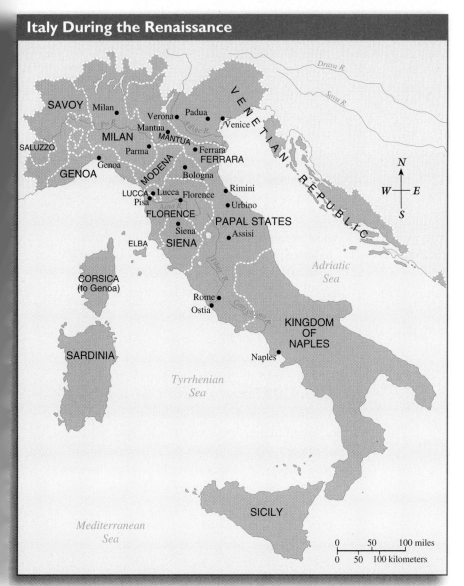

SAVOY
Milan
Verona
Padua
VENETIAN REPUBLIC
MILAN
Mantua
Venice
SALUZZO
Parma
MANTUA
Genoa
Ferrara
GENOA
MODENA
FERRARA
Bologna
LUCCA
Lucca
Rimini
Pisa
Florence
FLORENCE
Urbino
Siena
PAPAL STATES
ELBA
SIENA
Assisi
CORSICA
(to Genoa)
Adriatic
Sea
Rome
Ostia
KINGDOM
OF
NAPLES
SARDINIA
Naples
Tyrrhenian
Sea
SICILY
Mediterranean
Sea

Drava R.
Sava R.
Po R.
Adige R.

N
W E
S

0   50   100 miles
0   50   100 kilometers

state. These ambitions led to a higher educational standard and a broader definition of what it meant to be educated. Merchants wanted their sons to know how to keep good business records. They also wanted them to know the law and to be skilled at negotiation and diplomacy so that they would know how to deal with their trading partners. Since these young men would be traveling around a lot, they also needed to learn history and geography. These merchants also wanted their sons to learn about religion and good morals. So some of them even wanted their sons to learn ancient Greek as well as Latin, so that they could read the best ancient books. This created jobs for humanists willing to work as tutors or schoolteachers, and helped spread their love of humanities through the city-states.

Italians came into contact with people from distant lands and of differing faiths. Some of these differences could be found close to home. While most Renaissance Italians were Christians, many city-states also included Jewish families. Business trips often sent Italian merchants to regions of northern Europe. Trade also brought them into contact with Muslims from the East and the South. Contact with Muslims was especially fruitful since, during the Middle Ages, Islamic scholars had preserved many Ancient Greek manuscripts.

> **vocabulary**
> **patron** a wealthy person who supports an artist

other lands. Competition among the city-states led to further improvements, as each city-state worked hard to attract the best traders.

As trade grew, a new merchant class sprang up in the more prosperous city-states. Many merchants grew wealthy, and some of them used their wealth to support humanistic scholarship and the arts. Wealthy merchants, as well as aristocrats and churchmen, who supported the arts were known as **patrons**. Without these patrons there probably would have been no Renaissance.

Members of the new merchant class were also eager to give their sons an education that would teach them how to be successful businessmen and good leaders who could help to run their city-

Islam also contributed to the Renaissance in a less direct way. As Islam expanded and the Muslim Turks began to take over lands that had previously been controlled by the Byzantine Empire, Byzantine scholars were displaced. Some of these scholars fled to Italy. They brought with them valuable Greek manuscripts, as well as something that was then a rarity in Italy—a thorough knowledge of the ancient Greek language in which the texts were written.

An Important Invention

Once the Renaissance began, it was greatly accelerated by an all-important invention that was made in Germany: the printing press. Around 1450, Johannes Gutenberg (yoh HAHN es GOOT en burg) developed an efficient way of printing with movable type. Gutenberg devised a system of movable letter stamps, which were inked and then pressed onto paper. This invention allowed numerous copies of the same publication to be produced quickly and cheaply. Prior to this invention, writings had to be copied by hand, a slow and expensive process. The humanists had been willing to copy manuscripts because they were so excited about their discoveries, but even the most energetic scholar could only make a handful of copies of any given manuscript.

Printing changed all that. It made it possible to share the knowledge the humanists had gathered by printing and distributing multiple copies. Use of movable type and the printing press spread quickly in Italy. By 1500, Italy boasted more printing presses than any other country in Europe. Printers such as the Manutius who Erasmus visited helped spread the important texts of ancient Greece and Rome far and wide.

The presence of ancient ruins, the prosperity of the Italian city-states, the rise of merchants and other wealthy patrons, increased interest in education, greater exposure to foreign cultures, an influx of Byzantine scholars toting Greek manuscripts, and the invention of the printing press—these are some of the factors that combined to initiate and accelerate the Italian Renaissance.

Because all of these changes were happening at about the same time, there was a feeling of excitement in the air. Erasmus gave voice to this excitement when he spoke of a new day dawning. A writer and government official in Florence captured the excitement of the Renaissance when he wrote that every man should "thank God that it has been permitted to him to be born in this new age, so full of hope and promise, which already rejoices in a greater array of nobly-gifted souls than the world has seen in the thousand years that have preceded it."

Knowledge spread because of print shops such as the one pictured here, which could produce many volumes in a short time.

The Artist Elevated When we visit an art museum, we are not surprised to notice that an artist has signed his or her work by painting a name on the canvas or chiseling it into stone. Nor are we surprised that a museum might advertise an exhibit of artwork created by a particular artist.

We do not find it unusual that the architect's name is cut into the cornerstone of a building. When we hear a piece of music, we usually also expect to learn who composed it.

But it was not always that way. Before the Renaissance, painters did not generally sign their works, architects did not typically carve their names on the buildings they built, and musicians were rarely given credit for music they composed.

In the medieval period, artists did not have the status that they enjoy today. They were considered artisans or craftspersons. Painters and sculptors worked with their hands, like shoemakers or bakers or bricklayers, and they often worked for low wages, just as other craftspersons did. A medieval artist created precisely the work his employer paid him to produce, and he didn't even think of signing it.

The relatively low status of sculptors and painters was evident from the guilds, or trade associations, to which they belonged. Sculptors, for example, were members of the Guild of Masons, because, like **masons**, they worked with stone. Painters were members of the Guild of Doctors and Apothecaries because they depended on **apothecaries** (uh PATH uh ker eez) for many of their paints and supplies.

A Change of Status

During the Renaissance, however, the status of artists changed dramatically. The humanists discovered that the ancient Greeks and Romans had great respect for artists and architects; and when beautiful Greek and Roman statues were put on display, people began to see why. People began to feel that if artists could create such beautiful objects, then an artist must be something much greater than a baker or a bricklayer.

The humanists also unearthed manuscripts that described forgotten artistic techniques and showed artists how to use mathematical principles to give form and structure to their works. Artists mastered these techniques and principles, imitated the ancient works that had been recovered, and created impressive works of their own.

Gradually, a change began to take place. Painters and sculptors began to think of themselves as artists rather than just artisans, as creators rather than just craftspersons. They began taking credit for their creations by signing them. The best artists also began to charge handsome fees, particularly in the late fifteenth and early sixteenth centuries. A few great artists even felt free to change or ignore their patrons' directions. This did not always create good will between the patron and the artist. But it says something about the rising confidence and status of artists. If they lost the patronage of one leading family, they could hope for work from another.

> **vocabulary**
> **mason** a person who builds or works with brick or stone
> **apothecary** a druggist or pharmacist

Some painters and sculptors even took to inserting likenesses of themselves in their works. Lorenzo Ghiberti (loh REN tsoh gee BER tee) a successful bronze sculptor in Florence in the first half of the fifteenth century, included a self-portrait in one of the magnificent doors he created for the famous Baptistery of the cathedral in Florence. Sandro Botticelli (SAHN droh baht uh CHEL ee), a fifteenth-century painter from Florence, painted himself in one of his paintings of the *Adoration of the Magi*. In the painting Botticelli stands to one side, looking straight out at the viewer.

Artists were not alone in exhibiting themselves through artwork. Prominent men commissioned portraits and busts of themselves. Important families engaged artists to create works that would memorialize family members. In the Renaissance many people began to display a heightened awareness of themselves as unique individuals.

The Renaissance was, in many ways, a self-conscious age. Erasmus believed humankind was undergoing a fundamental change. Renaissance artists and their patrons were interested in themselves, their social standing, and their own special personalities. Their medieval counterparts would have been astounded by this focus on the individual self.

Portrait Painting

This heightened awareness of one's self as a unique individual went hand in hand with an increased emphasis on realism in art. Medieval painters had paid relatively little attention to realistic detail; the figures in their pictures were identifiable as human beings, but they generally didn't look like anyone in particular. They were symbols. Renaissance artists, with their new interest in the individual, began to strive for increased realism. They wanted their portraits to capture the exact appearance of a particular person in a particular situation. They wanted the figures in their portraits to have distinct facial expressions revealing emotions that viewers could understand. People in these paintings must seem to live and breathe, just like people in real life. To arouse the viewers' emotions, the picture must be dramatic.

Botticelli's Adoration of the Magi *shows wise men visiting the baby Jesus (center), but it also includes a self-portrait of the artist (lower right).*

The Natural World

Renaissance painters also began to pay more attention to the natural world. Most medieval art was made for churches and other religious settings. Both painters and their patrons liked to fill the spaces around the figures in their paintings with gold leaf, to show their love and respect for the figures and stories in these paintings. They wanted just enough detail so that anyone who saw the work of art would know easily what it was about. By the time the Renaissance reached its full bloom, people wanted paintings that looked lively and more like the world around them. They also wanted paintings that showed off the skill and creativity of the artist.

The painter and architect Brunelleschi (broo nel LES kee), who worked in Florence and Rome in the early fifteenth century, made one of the most important advances on the road to more realistic depiction of life. Brunelleschi was inspired by an essay on architecture written by an ancient Roman writer named Vitruvius (vih TROO vee us). Vitruvius described how buildings and other objects painted on a flat surface could be made to "advance and recede" so the painting would look more realistic and almost three dimensional. Brunelleschi applied what he read to a drawing he made of the public square in front of the cathedral of Florence. In doing so, he rediscovered the technique of **perspective.**

Brunelleschi taught the principles of perspective to a young Florentine painter named Masaccio (mah SAHT choh). Masaccio, and after him many other Renaissance painters, mastered perspective and used it to produce magnificent, realistic art. Renaissance painters were now able to place realistic figures in realistic backgrounds; indeed, they began to create spaces so realistic that viewers felt they could step through the painting into the world depicted.

Brunelleschi's rediscovery of perspective was a good example of how Renaissance artists managed to go forward by looking backward. Brunelleschi learned what he could from the ancient writers and then used what he had learned to improve his own art. By devoting himself to realism and teaching others how to use the principles of perspective, he helped foster a new appreciation for art and paved the way for a great flowering of the arts in Florence.

vocabulary
perspective a technique that allows artists to show objects as they appear at various distances from the viewer, with distant objects shown smaller and nearby objects larger

Notice the difference between the flat feeling of this medieval painting of the Adoration and the use of perspective in Botticelli's work.

he City on the Arno To experience all the wonders of the Renaissance, one only had to visit the city of Florence in the 1400s. Its economy, artists, architects, writers, and philosophers all helped make Florence a model of Renaissance culture.

Florence was well situated to become a center of trade and commerce. Like other important Italian cities of that age, Florence enjoyed important geographic advantages. It had been founded in Roman times on flatland alongside the River Arno. To the west, the river gave it access to the sea. The city was accessible in other directions through a variety of mountain passes.

By the time of the Renaissance, Florence had grown large, rich, and, in comparison with other Italian city-states, politically stable. Like other cities, Florence was by no means free from violence. Nor was it free from the filth caused by inadequate sewage systems. In contrast to many other cities, however, its commercial success and its form of government allowed the city to overcome these handicaps and enabled some of its richer citizens to make lasting contributions to Western civilization.

Near the height of its influence in 1472, the city of Florence boasted a powerful merchant class that was the envy of rival city-states. One Florentine silk merchant self-importantly declared, "A Florentine who is not a merchant, who has not traveled through the world, seeing foreign nations and peoples and then returned to Florence with some wealth, is a man who enjoys no esteem whatsoever."

Florence became best known in history for its painters, sculptors, architects, and scholars. But these artistic successes depended on the city's commercial successes, since it was the wealthy Florentine merchants who served as patrons and made the flowering of the arts possible.

Florence became an intellectual center as well. The leading men in Florence turned to the study of ancient Roman authors. These classical writers told a story of great political, commercial, and military accomplishments that appealed to the rising merchant class. An appreciation of classical civilization developed in Florence. This helped create an atmosphere in which bold political and artistic ideas could grow and flourish.

Wool and Banking

Florence's wealth during the Renaissance was heavily dependent on two industries: wool and banking. It is estimated that at the wool industry's peak, about one-third of Florentines worked in the wool business. The names of the city's streets testify to wool's importance. There were, for example, the Street of Shearers, the Street of Cauldrons (giant pots in which wool was cleaned and treated), and the Road of Dyers. Each of them was dedicated to a process required to turn raw wool into the cloth that Florentine merchants sold throughout the world.

The leading Florentine merchants involved in the wool business were members of the Wool Guild and the Calimala Guild. Members of the Calimala trade association controlled the importing, dyeing, and finishing of cloth. This guild was the most important and powerful of the greater guilds of Florence. Many cloth merchants also were members of the Guild of Bankers and Moneychangers. Quite often it was these influential families who ran the government of Florence.

The structure of the government of Florence was complex. Inspired by the example of Greece and Rome, Florence considered itself a **republic**.

In those times, that meant that power was in the hands of a ruling class of citizens rather than a single monarch. About 800 leading families in Florence were responsible for electing the city's government officials. The citizens were governed by a council composed of rich and educated men who represented the people.

A Powerful Family

Banking made a few merchants as rich and as powerful as the nobility for the first time in history. Imitating the nobility, these bankers and merchants became patrons of the arts.

No Florentine family was more rich and powerful than the Medici (MED uh chee) family. The Medici were wool merchants who rose to prominence largely on the basis of their banking business. By 1417 the family had bank branches in several important cities in Italy as well as in other key European cities. Perhaps most important, the Medici were the moneylenders to the pope, the leader of Christians in Europe. They enjoyed a most profitable relationship with the papal office responsible for collecting and spending church revenues.

In 1429, Cosimo de' Medici assumed leadership of the Medici family, upon the death of his father. Like his father, Cosimo possessed a genius for

banking. In time, the government of Florence came to depend on the Medici banking operation for the generous loans it made.

Cosimo soon became the leading citizen of the republic. He rarely held government office himself, but he was able to ensure that his friends often held office. Through them he maintained effective control of the government.

The education Cosimo received during his youth had nourished in him a deep respect for the ancient civilizations of Greece and Rome. From his youth, Cosimo paid agents to search for manuscripts abroad. He employed a staff of about 45 men to copy for his library any manuscripts he was unable to purchase.

> **vocabulary**
> **republic** a system of government in which voters elect officials to run the government and make laws

Later in life he would demonstrate his respect for the civilizations of Greece and Rome by spending large sums of his family's money on classical art and architecture. He funded many architects, sculptors, and painters, including the architect Brunelleschi, who, as we have seen, rediscovered the technique of perspective. Among Brunelleschi's most important works was the dome of the Santa Maria del Fiore (SAN tuh mah REE uh del FYOH ree) cathedral in Florence, often called the Duomo (DWOH moh).

Building of the cathedral was begun in 1294, and many great artists and sculptors worked on the church before it was completed in 1436.

You can appreciate why it took more than 100 years to build the great cathedral in Florence.

In 1415, Brunelleschi was given responsibility for designing and building the dome for the church. The sculptor planned to build a large stone dome. But daringly, Brunelleschi built the dome without interior supports to hold up the heavy stone and bricks. Brunelleschi obviously understood enough about structural design to recognize that the dome would be stable without using supports. Brunelleschi became known as the first genius of the Renaissance. His dome was considered the greatest engineering feat of the time.

Upon Cosimo de' Medici's death in 1464, his son Piero assumed leadership of the famous family. Piero lived only five years more. He was succeeded by his son Lorenzo, who became known as Lorenzo the Magnificent.

Lorenzo the Magnificent

Lorenzo de' Medici strove to make Florence a center of festivals, pageants, and processions. He commissioned artists to create works for himself and for the public spectacles he organized. But he was most influential in encouraging other prominent men to hire the city's artists.

During nine years of relative peace and prosperity, Lorenzo de' Medici was able to exert political influence, as his grandfather had. But in 1478 he was the victim of a plot hatched by a rival family in Florence. The plan was apparently backed by Pope Sixtus IV. Lorenzo survived an assassination attempt and a subsequent war with the pope's forces. When he returned to Florence in 1480, he determined that nothing like that would happen to him again. So he surrounded

The Medici were the richest family in Italy. Under Cosimo, shown here, they became a powerful political force.

himself with armed guards and took control of the government—becoming, in effect, the sole ruler.

For the next 12 years, Lorenzo concentrated on making Florence Italy's capital of art and learning. He brought the most famous teachers of Italy to the city-state. He spent large sums on art and books. He founded a school to provide boys with training, not only in art but also in the humanities. The sculptor, architect, and painter Michelangelo spent four years in Lorenzo's school. Michelangelo became a member of the Medici household and showed his patron the results of his work each day.

Unfortunately, Lorenzo did not have the same interest in the Medici's banking business or the same business skills as his grandfather. As a result, the bank's fortunes declined, and so did the fortunes of the city of Florence. Trade with the East decreased. The city's cloth merchants found themselves unable to compete with cloth merchants in Flanders, in present-day Belgium. Florence's role as a center of art and learning did not end, but other cities were better able to compete with it.

Lorenzo died in 1492. He was succeeded by his son Piero, who was forced into exile two years later. The Medicis returned to power in Florence in 1512. But it was not only as rulers of Florence that the family continued to influence the course of the Renaissance. Lorenzo had arranged for his son Giovanni (joh VAHN ee) to be named a cardinal in the church. Giovanni would eventually become Pope Leo X. And it was in Rome that Leo X was able to promote the splendor of Renaissance art and learning.

The Splendor of the Popes Popes occupied a unique and powerful place in Renaissance Italy, indeed in the world. They considered themselves the successors of St. Peter, one of the 12 apostles of Jesus and the first leader of the Christian Church.

It was a pope's responsibility to lead the Christian Church, to shepherd the believers whom Jesus had referred to as "my flock." The popes managed the largest organization in Europe—the Roman Catholic Church.

The popes were rulers of a large part of Italy called the Papal States. The territories they ruled had been given to them over the course of many centuries. By the time of the Renaissance, the popes ruled the largest kingdom in Italy except for the Kingdom of Naples. They governed these territories from the Vatican, the center of the Papal States, located in Rome. They believed the territories gave them political independence.

Pope Nicholas V is the pope who is usually credited with bringing Renaissance thinking to Rome. Nicholas was a dedicated humanist. He made teachers, historians, and thinkers welcome in Rome. He rebuilt and repaired many of the city's buildings and bridges and hired artists to increase their magnificence. In that way he made Rome more hospitable to tourists and pilgrims, who helped fill the treasuries of the church and of Roman merchants.

Among Pope Nicholas's successors, some eagerly accepted humanism and others rejected it. Pope Sixtus IV improved Rome's roads and buildings, added more than a thousand books to the Vatican library, built the Sistine Chapel in the Vatican, and brought the best artists to Rome to add to its beauty.

The Papal States also coined money. This coin bears the likeness of Pope Innocent XIII.

Pope Julius II, like his uncle Sixtus IV, was much involved in worldly matters. He was a brilliant administrator and an effective military leader. Julius II managed to reassert authority over the Papal States, which had been weakened under the reign of a predecessor.

Also like his uncle, Julius II expanded the Vatican library. To celebrate the church's glory and its teachings, he invited important artists to come to Rome to apply their skills to existing church properties and to create and beautify new ones. He hired the young painter Raphael to paint **frescoes** on the walls of the papal apartments. Julius II also hired Michelangelo, first to design his tomb and then to paint the ceiling of the Sistine Chapel.

The artists that Julius II brought to Rome were influenced by their exposure to antiquity in this ancient capital of the Roman Empire. It inspired them to create works whose beauty and nobility are still recognized today.

St. Peter's Basilica

For 1,200 years a church had stood on the site where it was believed that St. Peter had been buried. In 1506, under Pope Julius II, workers began building a magnificent new **basilica** to replace the original church.

> **vocabulary**
> **fresco** a painting made on fresh, moist plaster with color pigments dissolved in water
> **basilica** a Christian church building, often in the shape of a cross

*The Square in front of St. Peter's was built to hold the huge crowds
that came, and still come, for important papal ceremonies.*

St. Peter's Basilica was not completed for 120 years. Great artists, such as Michelangelo and Raphael, applied their skills to this massive design and construction project. The Church and Renaissance artists worked together to create one of the most remarkable and beautiful buildings in the world. This project also confirmed the importance of the Church.

Julius was succeeded by Lorenzo de' Medici's son Giovanni, who took the name Leo X. Leo X was elected pope in 1513, the year after his family was restored to power in Florence. As pope, he showed both a love of art and a love of luxury. Like his father, Leo encouraged and sponsored festivals, pageants, and processions, starting with his own magnificent coronation ceremonies. He hired the best artists, including both Michelangelo and Raphael, and welcomed scholars and poets to the Vatican.

Leo's efforts to increase the splendor of Rome were expensive, especially the continuing construction of St. Peter's Basilica. To pay the immense costs, Leo X raised taxes and borrowed huge sums. Like the popes before him, he approved the sale of positions of authority in the Church. And, in 1514, he extended throughout much of Europe a campaign that Julius II had limited to Italy: the sale of the so-called St. Peter's indulgences. Leo X promised that contributors to the building fund would receive special spiritual benefits and that the punishment that God would impose for their previous misdeeds would be lifted. This practice would help trigger what was later called the *Protestant Reformation*, which resulted in divisions in the Christian Church that remain unhealed. (You will learn more about the Reformation after you finish reading about the Renaissance.)

Although Leo's goal was noble, the way he went about reaching his goal was not so noble. This mixture of honorable purpose and question-able ways of achieving the purpose came to char-acterize much of Renaissance Rome.

Last of the Renaissance Popes

Clement VII, the nephew of Lorenzo de' Medici and a cousin of Pope Leo X, became pope in 1523. Clement shared his family's love of the arts. But Clement proved unable to make wise decisions in the alliances he made to ensure the independence of the Papal States. Enemies attacked Rome in 1527. They looted churches and monasteries and destroyed many manuscripts in the Vatican library. They damaged some of the artwork the popes had commissioned, including one of Raphael's frescoes in the papal apartments.

Clement made peace with his enemies and was returned to power in 1528. But Rome never returned to its position as the center of the Renaissance. Its intellectual and artistic leaders had been scattered. Never again would such an impressive attempt be made to join Christianity with the values and ideals of classical antiquity.

Glittering City "You should visit Venice if you want other cities to seem like poorhouses," a prominent resident once told a friend. Built on 117 small islands, Venice, in northern Italy, was the western world's foremost commercial city in 1500.

Venice's islands, located in the middle of a **lagoon,** were divided by more than 150 canals and connected by more than 400 bridges. Many of its buildings rested on pillars driven into the mud. Venice was safe from an attack. Enemy ships found it impossible to move in the shallow waters. Venice also had a strong navy which was the foundation of its considerable wealth.

The people of Venice, called Venetians (vuh NEE shunz), were proud of their splendid city. Visitors also shared their admiration. A French diplomat visiting Venice painted a glowing picture of this unusual city. "The houses are very large and lofty and built of stone," he reported. "Within they have, most of them . . . rich marble chimney pieces, bedsteads of gold color, their portals [doors] of the same, and most gloriously furnished. In short, it is the most triumphant city that I have ever seen."

How did Venice gain its prosperity? Like Florence, Venice built its wealth primarily on trade. Over two centuries, the Venetians fashioned an extensive trading empire. They were not trying to gain territory over which to rule. Rather, the goal was to ensure that they could carry on their trading activities without interference.

vocabulary
lagoon a shallow body of water, especially one separated from a larger body of water by a sandbar or reef

Venice became the great maritime power of the Renaissance.

Venice wanted safe access by sea to ports in Syria and Egypt and along the coast of the Black Sea. There, Venetian merchants could purchase the herbs, spices, and dyes that originated in the Far East and the cottons, silks, and silver goods of the Middle East. There, too, they could offer in trade the many products of Venice's own industries, such as glass, textiles, and jewelry.

Therefore, during the thirteenth and fourteenth centuries, Venice established ports and island strongholds along the Adriatic Sea, leading to the Mediterranean Sea. They were defended by a formidable navy, whose flat-bottomed **galleys** were built in Venice. This shipbuilding enterprise employed about 2,000 workers and probably was the largest industry of its time.

Venice also wanted free access to its trading partners north of the Alps. So, during the fifteenth century, Venice conquered mainland territories to its north and west, including Padua (PAJ oŏ uh) and Verona (vuh ROH nuh) in present-day Italy. These conquests assured safe overland passage for goods that Venetian merchants wanted to sell in Germany and elsewhere in northern Europe.

vocabulary
galley a large, flat-bottomed ship propelled by sails and oars and used in the Mediterranean for trade and war

Late in the fifteenth century and early in the sixteenth, Venice suffered some military setbacks, however. First, Turkish forces seized many of Venice's eastern territories. The Turks forced Venice to pay a yearly fee for trading in Turkish ports. Then, an alliance of Italian, German, French, and Spanish forces, headed by Pope Julius II, recaptured some of the mainland Italian territories Venice had conquered. (See the map of the Italian city-states.) Within a few years, Venice won back part of these possessions, though at great financial and human cost.

Its efficient navy gave Venice the military force it needed to defend a substantial empire. Its distinctive form of government gave it the stability it needed to establish and maintain this empire.

Republican Government

Venice, like Florence, was not a monarchy but a republic whose government was controlled by the city-state's leading families. The head of the government was called the doge (dohj), which comes from a Latin word meaning "leader." The doge was chosen for life by members of the Greater Council. This council also selected from its members those who would serve in other governmental bodies, including a senate and a committee for public safety. Although the doge was Venice's chief of state, real power lay in the hands of the council and the other governmental bodies whose members it selected.

As in most other republics up to that time, not all Venetians could participate in government. At the end of the thirteenth century, the Greater Council passed a law that said only male descendants of men who had sat in the council before 1297 were allowed to be members. The name of everyone eligible was written down in what became known as the *Book of Gold*. Only about 200 families were named in the book. They became hereditary rulers of Venice.

In the late fifteenth and early sixteenth centuries, the wealth its merchant traders amassed allowed Venice to compete with Florence and Rome for leadership of the Renaissance.

Aside from its wealth, Venice relied on an additional resource—displaced scholars. In 1453 many persecuted scholars fled Constantinople, the capital of the Byzantine Empire, after it was conquered by Muslim Turks. They began to make their way into Europe. A notable number of them moved to Venice. They brought not only their knowledge but also their precious manuscripts from Ancient Greece.

As in Florence and Rome, architects, scholars, and artists patronized by wealthy Venetians made lasting contributions to Western civilization. Some of Venice's most remarkable buildings, such as the Basilica of St. Mark and the Palace of the Doges, had already been constructed by the time of the Renaissance. But Renaissance architects left their mark in the new buildings they designed and the styles they created during this period.

Printing Advances

Venice made an especially notable contribution to classical learning by encouraging the development of the new craft of printing. By 1500 this city-state alone had more than 200 printing presses. Because many printers were scholars, they devoted themselves to searching out and publishing classical manuscripts, particularly those of Ancient Greece.

The printer whom Erasmus visited in Venice, Aldus Manutius, was so dedicated to his craft that he placed a notice over the door of his office: "Whoever you are, you are earnestly requested by Aldus to state your business briefly and to take your departure promptly. For this is a place of work." Aldus Manutius later died exhausted and poor, but he had succeeded in enriching his own age and ages to come by using this new means to preserve an ancient heritage.

Venice's Greatest Artist

Of all the arts for which Renaissance Venice became known, painting was the foremost. No Venetian painter was more respected for his artistry than Tiziano Vecelli (tee SYAH noh vay CHEL lee), known in history as Titian (TIHSH un). Born about 1488, he was brought to Venice at age nine or ten to study with some of the city's most important painters. When his long career came to an end in 1576, he had surpassed them all.

This portrait of Isabella d'Este, a prominent woman of the Renaissance, shows how Titian was able to make the viewer aware of the luxury of her dress, furs, and jewels.

Titian was noted for his appeal to the emotions and senses rather than to the mind. His use of color and his pioneering use of oil paints gave his works a rich and luxurious feel. Among Titian's most famous paintings is *The Assumption of the Virgin*, a powerful, exciting work showing the Virgin Mary being taken to heaven.

Although most Venetians admired Titian's work, not everyone agreed. Michelangelo, for example, admired Titian's "coloring and style." But he noted, "It was a pity good design was not taught in Venice."

Also famous is Titian's series of portraits of the Holy Roman Emperor Charles V, who became his patron, as well as portraits of Francis I of France and Philip II of Spain. So much did Emperor Charles V admire Titian that, it is reported, he once picked up the artist's paintbrush when Titian dropped it on the floor—something unheard of for an emperor to do for a mere commoner!

Decline of Venice

Even during its golden age of art and learning, Venice was already losing ground as the foremost trading power of the world. The Muslim Turks had successfully challenged Venetian dominance in the Mediterranean. New sea routes to the Far East discovered by Portuguese explorers would turn trade away from the Mediterranean and the Middle East to the Atlantic Ocean and beyond. Venice would remain an independent state until the end of the eighteenth century. But it would never again exercise the central role in world trade and commerce that it held in the glory days of the Renaissance.

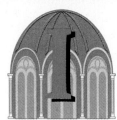

Imagining Things That Are to Be A young man named Leonardo da Vinci applied for a job with the ruling duke of Milan (mih LAN). To convince the duke of his worth, Leonardo sent a lengthy description of the services he could offer. Today, we would call the description his résumé.

"I have plans for bridges, very light and strong and suitable for carrying very easily," he wrote. "When a place is besieged I know how to cut off water from the trenches and how to construct . . . scaling ladders and other instruments." He went on to describe his plans for destroying fortresses, constructing various "engines" for attack and defense, and making cannons and armored cars.

If we knew nothing else about him but his description of what he could do, we might think him an engineer or a soldier. In fact, he was also one of the foremost artists of the age, indeed of any age.

Like many great Renaissance artists, Leonardo was a jack-of-all-trades. He was a sculptor, a painter, a designer, and a scientist. Most of all, he was a visionary.

Leonardo was born in 1452 near the village of Vinci, about 60 miles from Florence. When he was about 15, his father took him to a famous artist in Florence. He persuaded the artist to make his son an **apprentice**.

Apprentices observed the master at work and did whatever menial tasks he gave them. Gradually, they began to learn how to work at the various branches of painting, designing, and sculpting under the master.

Apprentices' work was demanding. They rarely had days off. They spent long hours copying drawings so they would become familiar with the master's style. In fact, although a painting bore the master's name, it was quite possible that an apprentice actually had completed the work.

Leonardo spent less time as an apprentice than most boys. And, as time would demonstrate, he was spectacularly talented. A story is told that once Leonardo was assigned to paint an angel in one of his master's commissioned paintings. When the master saw what Leonardo

vocabulary

apprentice in the Middle Ages and the Renaissance, someone who agreed to live with and work for another for a specified period, in return for instruction in a trade or craft

Leonardo da Vinci drew this self portrait when he was an old man.

had done, he found it so beautiful he knew that he could never equal it. The master then gave up painting to concentrate on sculpture. The story may be a legend, but it serves to emphasize what later became apparent to the world: Leonardo da Vinci was an artist of rare ability.

About five years after he began his apprenticeship, Leonardo established his own workshop in Florence. Leonardo completed some remarkable work during this time. But he also began a habit of starting works that he would not complete.

The Master of All Trades

Leonardo was about 30 years old when he sent his résumé to the duke of Milan. He had heard that the duke was looking for a military engineer, a painter, an architect, and a sculptor. Leonardo offered himself as all four in one person. The duke would not be disappointed.

During his 17-year stay in Milan, Leonardo completed some of his greatest work. After he arrived in Milan, the duke asked him to paint on the wall of a monastery dining room a picture of the Last Supper. This represented the final meal Jesus shared with his twelve apostles. The artist labored for three years on the project. It was said that the **prior** complained that the artist was taking too much time to complete the work.

When the duke asked Leonardo why it was taking so long, the artist explained that he was having trouble painting the faces of Jesus and of the apostle Judas, who would betray Jesus. He could not imagine how to paint a face so beautiful that it was worthy of Jesus, nor could he imagine how to paint the features of a man as horrible as Judas. He cunningly suggested to the duke that he might use the face of the prior as a model for Judas. Word must have gotten back to the prior because, from that time on, Leonardo was able to work at his painting without any complaints from the prior.

When Leonardo completed *The Last Supper*, it was recognized as a masterpiece. The painting remains in its original place today, but it has suffered greatly over the years from dampness, neglect, and natural deterioration. Nonetheless, many people feel it is the greatest painting that the Renaissance produced up to that point.

These pages from Leonardo's notebooks show how keen his mind was and how varied his interests were.

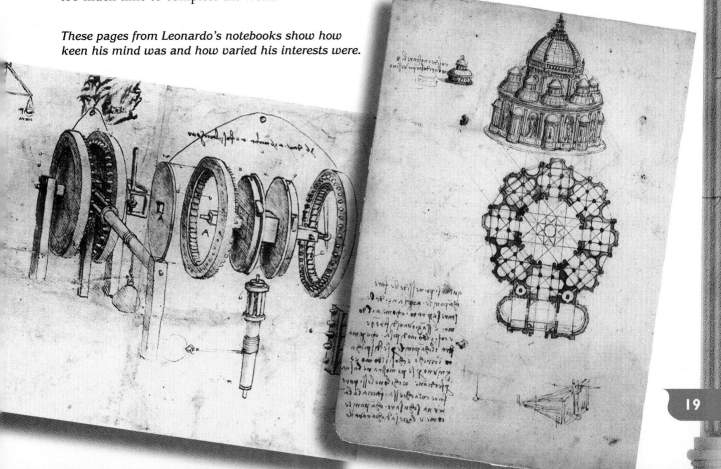

True to his résumé, Leonardo applied himself in many fields. He designed a device that allowed a person to study the total eclipse of the sun without damaging the eye. He designed the first parachute. He designed a model city with two levels and a series of underground canals. An accomplished musician, he even invented musical instruments, such as mechanized drums and keyboards for wind instruments.

Leonardo spent countless hours observing nature, drawing and recording in many notebooks what he saw. He also studied mathematics because he believed it was the foundation of art. One of his famous drawings illustrates a formula that states that the span of a man's outstretched arms is equal to his height.

Beyond Milan

In 1499, France captured Milan. Leonardo moved first to the safety of Mantua (MAN choo wuh) and then to Venice, where he worked as a naval engineer. In 1500 he returned to Florence. Except for a year during which he worked for a powerful military leader, he remained in Florence until 1506.

During this period he completed his other most famous painting, and perhaps the most famous portrait in the world, the *Mona Lisa*. The painting portrays the wife of a prominent Florentine citizen. For centuries since, viewers have been attracted by the artist's use of light and shade, his attention to detail in the woman's clothing, and his use of an invented landscape as background. Viewers were fascinated by the woman's gaze and smile. What was she thinking? People today still ask that question as they file past the painting now displayed in the great Louvre (loov) museum in Paris.

Some people say that the Mona Lisa *is so lifelike that her eyes seem to follow a viewer across a room.*

Leonardo returned to Milan. He continued his artistic work there, but it became increasingly clear that science held his interest as well as art. When Leo X became pope, Leonardo moved to Rome, where Leo provided him with lodgings and pay. Later, at the invitation of King Francis I, Leonardo left Italy for France, to become the "painter, engineer, and architect of the King." There, he remained, until his death in 1519 at the age of 67.

Leonardo left behind relatively few finished works of art: only about a dozen paintings and not one complete sculpture. He did leave many detailed and highly accurate drawings of human anatomy and of various mechanical devices. And he left more than 5,000 pages from his notebooks.

Leonardo may not have been the best painter, sculptor, engineer, or thinker of his time. But no one then, and perhaps no one since, has so effectively combined the skills of each calling. No one was more able to imagine what could be. He was in many ways the embodiment of the Renaissance, a true **Renaissance man**, devoted to knowledge and beauty in all its forms and expressions. Like so much else, this idea was borrowed from the ancient Roman civilization. The Romans had held all-around competence, or ability, in high esteem. They would certainly have admired Leonardo da Vinci.

> **vocabulary**
> **Renaissance man**
> one who is highly skilled and has broad interests in many or all of the arts and sciences

Staring at the Ceiling For four years the artist labored, often under trying conditions. Lying on his back on scaffolding he had erected, he slowly covered the ceiling's 5,000 square feet with scenes from the Old Testament. His patron was not pleased with the pace of his work.

In fact, one day the patron angrily whacked the artist with a cane and threatened to throw him off the scaffold if he did not speed up his work.

The artist had not even wanted to accept the commission, for he thought of himself as a sculptor, not a painter. But the money was very good, and his patron was not a man to be denied. He was the pope. So Michelangelo continued to labor on.

It took him four years to complete his work. But when he had finished, the demanding patron, Pope Julius II, had no grounds for displeasure. The artist, Michelangelo Buonarroti (bwoh nahr ROH tee), had created a work of unparalleled magnificence, the ceiling of the Sistine (SIS teen) Chapel in Rome.

Michelangelo was a master of many artistic abilities. He often protested that he was a sculptor, as if he could not be expected to succeed in any other artistic field. In fact, he also was a marvelous painter and an architect who changed the face of Rome.

Also like Leonardo, Michelangelo was born near Florence—23 years later—and apprenticed in an artist's workshop when he was a boy. In 1488, at the age of 13, Michelangelo entered the workshop of a well-known Florentine painter. He spent only one year there, learning how to mix paints, prepare backgrounds for paintings, create frescoes, and draw with precision. In the following year he accepted an invitation from Lorenzo de' Medici to join an academy Lorenzo had founded. There he studied the Medicis' rich collection of Greek and Roman statues and learned the techniques of sculpture. He associated with all the artists and humanist thinkers that Lorenzo had gathered around him.

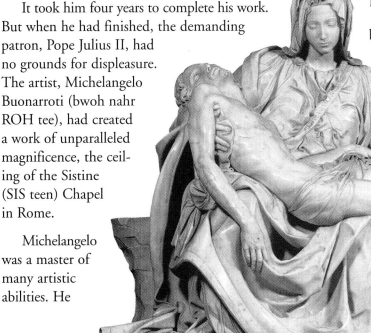

Many people consider this statue of the Pietà as Michelangelo's greatest sculpture. Every year thousands of visitors to St. Peter's in Rome admire this work.

To Rome

Four years after Lorenzo's death, Michelangelo moved to Rome. Like so many artists before him, he was fascinated by the ancient city's sculpture, architecture, and painting. He created his first major work in Rome, which made his reputation as a master sculptor. He was commissioned to create a large marble statue of Mary, the mother of Jesus, holding and mourning her dead son. A sculpture or painting of this scene is called a Pietà (pee ay TAH).

Michelangelo's extraordinarily lifelike Pietà was said to be the most beautiful work of marble in all of Rome. It remains in Rome today, and each year hundreds of thousands of visitors to St. Peter's Basilica continue to marvel at this magnificent sculpture.

The now-famous sculptor returned to Florence in 1501. There, he created a second masterwork from a colossal block of marble that had been discarded years earlier by another sculptor because it was flawed. It was an awe-inspiring statue of the young biblical hero David, who killed the giant Goliath. The statue almost seems alive. The artist's ability to overcome the imperfections of the marble to create this work marked him as the greatest sculptor of his age.

Four years later, Michelangelo was summoned back to Rome by Pope Julius II. Julius II wanted the artist to design and build a three-story tomb in which the pope would be buried. Thus began a peculiar love-hate relationship between the master artist and the demanding pope. The tomb was never completed as originally planned, because time and again Julius assigned new work for Michelangelo to do.

The Sistine Chapel

Many papal ceremonies were held in the Sistine Chapel. The pope gave Michelangelo the additional task of painting the ceiling. The artist designed the scaffolding, prepared the ceiling to be plastered—for this work was to be a fresco— and hired assistants to help him. In time he dismissed the assistants because he was dissatisfied with their work.

The Sistine Chapel is a huge space that took nearly four years to paint.

Michelangelo shut himself up in the huge room. He labored under extremely difficult conditions. When he climbed down at the end of a day's work, his back and neck ached, and his eyes were so used to focusing on a ceiling several feet away that he could not read a letter unless he held it at the same distance.

The finished work was a masterpiece. "There is no other work to compare with this for excellence, nor could there be," one artist wrote about Michelangelo's frescoes in the Sistine Chapel. The paintings depicted many scenes from the Old Testament, including the creation of Adam, the first man. The frescoes include more than 300 figures, some of them 18 feet high, and cover a space 118 feet long and 46 feet wide. The Sistine Chapel ceiling is Michelangelo's most famous work.

After Pope Julius died, Michelangelo stayed on in Rome under the new pope, Leo X. He had known this son of Lorenzo de' Medici in Florence. The artist continued work on the statues planned for Pope Julius's tomb. They included a monumental statue of Moses holding the tablets of the law, known as the Ten Commandments. The statue is found today in the Church of St. Peter in Chains, in Rome.

Return to Florence

In 1517, Michelangelo returned once again to Florence. The pope had asked him to design the facade, or front, of the Medici family church there. There were many problems with this project. Michelangelo not only had to train new workers to **quarry** the marble, but he also had to have a road built through the mountains to transport it. In time, the pope withdrew the commission. The artist had lost three years of work and was furious.

Nevertheless, when a new pope, Clement VII, was elected, Michelangelo agreed to stay in Florence and design the tombs of both Lorenzo de' Medici and his brother Giuliano (joo LYAH noh). He also agreed to design a library to be attached to the Medici church. His work was interrupted in 1527 when the troops of the Holy Roman emperor invaded Italy and sacked Rome. With Florence also in danger of attack, Michelangelo fled the city for Venice.

After order was restored, Michelangelo returned to Florence. He resumed his work on the library and tomb. Pope Clement asked him to return to the Sistine Chapel to paint the wall behind the altar. The pope died, however, as the artist was preparing to begin this work. The new pope, Paul III, named Michelangelo the chief painter, sculptor, and architect of the Vatican. He, too, asked the artist to paint the Sistine Chapel wall. As its theme the pope chose the Last Judgment, when all living and dead people would stand before God to be judged.

Last Judgment and Last Project

Michelangelo began the work, but it took him five years to complete it. He was 66 when he finished. The strain of the work took its toll on his health. Once, he fell off a scaffold, seriously injuring his leg.

The Last Judgment is a work of great power. The artist depicts Jesus both cursing the damned and welcoming the blessed. Its brown and orange colors, as well as the expressions and movements of Jesus and the other figures, give it a gloomy, even grim, feeling.

In 1546, Pope Paul III appointed Michelangelo, then 71 years old, chief architect for St. Peter's Basilica. His responsibilities included work on the exterior of the building as well as its dome, which became a model for domes throughout the western world.

The artist continued working almost until the day he died in 1564. When that day came, he remarked, "I regret that I am dying just as I am beginning to learn the alphabet of my profession."

Michelangelo was buried in Florence as he had wished. Michelangelo, who never married, left no children. His wife, he said, "was his art," and his children "the works I shall leave."

Daniele da Volterra, a sculptor who lived at the same time as Michelangelo, made this bronze bust of him.

23

Instructors in Manners In the Renaissance, as today, much advice was available in print regarding how to live and act. Today, many books and magazine articles claim to teach readers how to succeed in various areas of life. Such books also were available in the Renaissance. A number of them were widely read.

Many books of this type concentrated on basic matters. They were quite specific about behavior that was or was not acceptable. One of the most popular of such books, *The Book of Manners*, was published in 1558. The author advises:

- Refrain as far as possible from making noises which grate upon the ear, such as grinding or sucking your teeth.

- It is not polite to scratch yourself when you are seated at table.

- We should . . . be careful not to gobble our food so greedily as to cause ourselves to get hiccups or commit some other unpleasantness.

- You should neither comb your hair nor wash your hands in the presence of others—except for washing the hands before going in to a meal—such things are done in the bedroom and not in public.

The purpose of many of these books was to instruct the newly rich about behavior that would help them enter the social class above them. But another type of book did more than

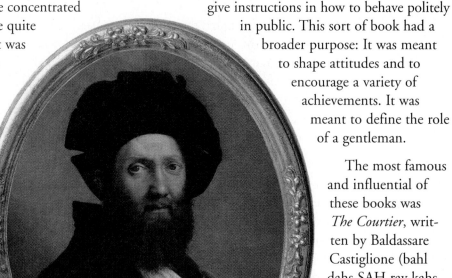

Raphael's portrait gives the impression that Castiglione would be an ideal courtier.

give instructions in how to behave politely in public. This sort of book had a broader purpose: It was meant to shape attitudes and to encourage a variety of achievements. It was meant to define the role of a gentleman.

The most famous and influential of these books was *The Courtier*, written by Baldassare Castiglione (bahl dahs SAH ray kahs tee LYOH nay). A courtier was an attendant in the court of a ruler. That is exactly what Castiglione was. He served as a soldier and **diplomat** in the court of the duke of Urbino (ur BEE noh).

By the time Castiglione joined the court at Urbino early in the sixteenth century, the hill town in central Italy had become known as a center of culture. The duke's court boasted one of the finest libraries of the time. A number of prominent artists, including the great painter Raphael, worked there. In fact, Raphael painted

vocabulary
diplomat one who represents a government in its relationships with other governments

a wonderful portrait of Castiglione, which now hangs in the Louvre museum in Paris.

How to Please Others

Castiglione's book was presented in the form of a series of conversations that supposedly took place at the court of Urbino. The conversations focused on what made men and women proper gentlemen and ladies.

The perfect courtier, according to the discussion, should be of noble birth, handsome, graceful, strong, and courageous. He should be skilled in war and in sports. Whatever he did, he should do it in such a way that it appeared "to be without effort."

The courtier, Castiglione and his companions decided, should have a high opinion of his own worth. He should not be afraid to advertise it to others but should do so in a way that did not appear boastful. So, he should ride near the front in processions to make sure he would be seen. He should try to accomplish his most daring feats where the ruler he served would notice him. He should not cheapen himself by mixing with people in social classes below him.

Machiavelli wrote a guide for rulers who wanted to create a lasting government.

The ideal courtier, according to Castiglione, also should be accomplished in learning. He should know Latin and Greek, be well read, and be able to write poetry and prose. He should appreciate painting, sculpture, music, and architecture, and be able to sing and dance gracefully.

Castiglione published his book in 1528. In a short time it was translated into French and English. It had a great influence for many years to come on standards of behavior and education, not only in Italy but also in France and England.

Today, it might seem as if the courtier the Italian diplomat described was all style and no substance. The ideal courtier of Renaissance Italy might strike us as someone more interested in making a good impression than in taking a stand. Castiglione argued that by developing the qualities he described, the ideal courtier would encourage his princely ruler to turn to him for advice. And by giving good advice, the courtier could exercise great influence in the way matters of government were decided.

How to Rule

Another important Renaissance writer argued strongly against this notion. In fact, he wrote, "It is an **infallible** rule that a prince who is not wise himself cannot be well-advised."

Niccolò Machiavelli (nee koh LOH mak ee uh VEL ee) lived and worked in and around Florence at the same time that Castiglione served in the court at Urbino. Like Castiglione, Machiavelli served as a diplomat, in his case for the government of Florence. From 1498 until 1512, Machiavelli held a number of positions in government. Each allowed him to observe how government worked or did not work. He was interested in how rulers gained and kept power.

Machiavelli was put in charge of the forces that were to defend Florence against armies headed by Pope Julius II. The

vocabulary
infallible incapable of error; certain

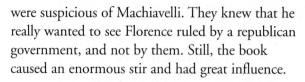

pope was angry that Florence had refused to help him expel French troops from Italy. He intended to put an end to the Florentine republic and restore the Medici family to rule.

Machiavelli's troops could not hold the line. The pope's forces took Florence, and the Medicis were returned to power. Machiavelli lost his government position, as well as his reputation. He went into exile on a small farm outside Florence. There, he spent most of his remaining years.

Advice for the Prince

The former diplomat long hoped for a return to government service. During his exile he wrote a small book of advice on how to govern, based on his own experience and study of history. If artists of the Renaissance drew their inspiration from the natural world, from the real shapes and forms they saw about them, Machiavelli did the same for politics. He looked at what happened in the actual world of power and government. He did not write about the ideal behavior of a Christian leader but of the actual behavior of present and past leaders. He called his most famous book *The Prince*, and many think of it as the first book of modern political science—the study of political institutions and how they work.

Machiavelli wrote the book hoping it would bring him to the attention of the Medicis. He wanted the Medicis to employ him once again in the city-state's government. That was not to be. In fact, the Medicis

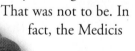

were suspicious of Machiavelli. They knew that he really wanted to see Florence ruled by a republican government, and not by them. Still, the book caused an enormous stir and had great influence.

The Prince was a total novelty. Because Machiavelli made no attempt to describe politics in a religious framework, he scandalized many. But he also described the workings of government very clearly, and rulers sat up and took notice.

Machiavelli agreed that, in general, it was praiseworthy for a prince "to keep his faith and to be an honest man." But he believed that a ruler might need to go back on his word in times of trouble or danger. Princes who acted boldly also won fame and glory, and that might be more valuable than keeping every promise. So he advised princes who wished to gain and maintain power "to learn how *not* to be good."

Like Castiglione, Machiavelli believed that appearances were important. A prince, he wrote, should be seen as "merciful, faithful, humane, sincere, religious." But he also wrote that when it served the ruler to be otherwise, he should "be able to change to the opposite qualities." Rulers, he insisted, sometimes had to use cunning, trickery, even cruelty, to get and keep power. "It is necessary for a prince who wishes to hold his own," Machiavelli wrote, "to know how to do wrong." Over the years many people have strongly disagreed with Machiavelli's judgments and directives. In fact, the term *Machiavellian* is still used to describe a person who is crafty and less than honest.

On the other hand, some scholars believe Machiavelli was simply being realistic. They say that his goal was to ensure the safety of the Florentine state. He believed any behavior that achieved this purpose was necessary, if not honorable. Machiavelli's defenders suggest that instead of writing a description of how an ideal Christian ruler should behave, he offered candid advice on ways efficient rulers should and did behave.

Lorenzo de' Medici looked like he could be the prince that Machiavelli described.

Spread of Spirit and Ideas Both *The Courtier* and *The Prince*, we have seen, had influence well beyond the borders of Italian city-states. Both books were translated into other languages. Both found willing readers in countries throughout Europe.

Translation of the printed word was just one of many ways in which the ideas and values of the Renaissance in Italy were spread through the rest of Europe.

The spirit and notions of the Renaissance also were carried outside Italy by Italian artists who traveled to other countries. Leonardo, for example, spent his final years in France as painter, engineer, and architect to King Francis I. Other Italian artists of the Renaissance also worked outside Italy, sharing their skills and ideals.

Visitors to Renaissance Italy often carried home respect for Italy's ancient civilization and its artistic discoveries and methods. Some visitors, such as Erasmus, came for learning. They found inspiration in Italy and gladly shared it with citizens of their home countries. Others, such as the invading German and French armies, came to conquer and steal. In many cases they were influenced by the cultural riches they found. They too carried their discoveries back, along with their loot.

Several factors had made Italy the center of the Renaissance in the fourteenth and fifteenth centuries: the closeness of Roman ruins, the geography and prosperity of the independent city-states, the rise of merchants

and patrons, and the reform of education. So too several factors came together elsewhere in the sixteenth century to open other countries to new learning and new possibilities.

Northern and Western Europe

In the 1500s some countries to the north and west of Italy developed well-organized central governments. The center of trade shifted from

Europe During the Renaissance

The influence of Renaissance Italy spread to the nation states of northern and western Europe in the 1500s.

the Mediterranean to the Atlantic, bringing some of these countries new wealth. Royal courts in France, England, and Germany supported young artists. New wealth also allowed a thriving merchant class to become patrons of art and learning.

Most of all, in these countries, as in Italy, there arose scholars and artists of genius. Many of them began by imitating the Italians, but eventually they made their own unique contributions to Western culture.

The German-speaking countries of the Holy Roman Empire to the north of Italy were among the first to welcome Renaissance values and ideals. Men like Erasmus helped spread humanism in those countries. The German Renaissance soon became caught up in religious disputes between Catholics and Protestants that we call the Reformation. Nevertheless, it produced a number of important scholars and artists.

Perhaps the greatest German painter of this period was Albrecht Dürer (AHL brekt DU rur), born in 1471. His goldsmith father took him to his workshop to teach him the trade. But the father soon discovered that his son had a remarkable talent for drawing. He apprenticed him to a local artist, where young Dürer quickly mastered the technique of designing woodcuts. These were blocks of wood carved and inked and used for printing illustrations.

After he finished his apprenticeship, Dürer traveled to France. There he improved the engraving skills he had learned in his father's goldsmith shop. Engravings were images carved onto metal plates with a sharp tool. The plates were then inked for printing. Dürer was to do some of his finest work as an engraver and woodcutter.

Dürer's self portrait shows a young man who is sure of his ability as an artist.

Dürer traveled to Italy for the first time. He visited Venice and there discovered new artistic styles and new forms of expression that were quite different from anything he had experienced in his native country. While in Venice he copied the paintings of well-known artists to improve his technique. He also studied mathematics, read poetry, and carefully observed the landscapes and life that surrounded him.

After Dürer returned to Germany, he established his own workshop. He soon became enormously popular, both as a painter and as an engraver. Two of his most remarkable paintings were self-portraits. On the second of them he wrote the following message in Latin: "Albrecht Dürer from Nuremberg, painted this myself with incredible colors at the age of twenty-eight years." Dürer's inscription is an example of the new confidence that artists acquired during the Renaissance. By using the word *incredible*, Dürer seems to be marveling at his own achievement and boasting that he is a man with a special gift.

Dürer painted and drew many other portraits, including one of Erasmus. But he was especially interested in creating engravings and woodcuts. Among his best works of this type is a series of engravings based on the Book of the Apocalypse in the Christian New Testament.

The Renaissance in France

The Renaissance flourished in France in the middle of the sixteenth century. Invasions of Italy by French troops introduced French leaders to Renaissance culture. What they saw amazed them. Earlier you read about how King Francis I hired Leonardo da Vinci to come to Paris to be "painter, engineer, and architect of the King."

Francis and the kings who followed him began to purchase Italian Renaissance paintings and sculpture. They also succeeded in bringing other Italian Renaissance artists to France.

French monarchs also built a series of lavish **chateaux** (sha TOH), designed by Italian architects and decorated in Renaissance style.

The influence of the Italian Renaissance did not stop there. Life in the chateaux was modeled on life in Italian courts, as described by Castiglione in *The Courtier*.

The Renaissance in England

In England the Renaissance reached its height in the late sixteenth and early seventeenth centuries. In many European countries it was the sculptors, painters, and architects who made the greatest contributions to the Renaissance. In England it was the writers.

During this period a number of notable poets and playwrights wrote works that are still read, performed, and loved today. Among them was William Shakespeare, often called the greatest playwright of all time. Shakespeare was born in Stratford-upon Avon in 1564. Before he was 30, he had moved to London. There he established himself as both a playwright and a poet.

There is no record that Shakespeare ever visited Italy. But the influence of Italy and the Italian Renaissance is apparent in a great many of his plays. *The Merchant of Venice* is a drama about a merchant in Renaissance Venice, while *Othello* is a tragedy about a general in the same city. *Romeo and Juliet* takes place in Verona. Many of his plots were taken from famous Italian stories.

> **vocabulary**
> **chateau** a French castle, or large country house; *chateaux* is the plural form

Shakespeare also shared the Renaissance interest in classical Greece and Rome. He wrote several plays about Ancient Greece and four tragedies about Ancient Rome, including *Julius Caesar* and *Antony & Cleopatra*.

Even when he was not writing about Renaissance Italy or the classical world, Shakespeare wrote like a man of the Renaissance. We saw earlier how he made Prince Hamlet speak like a Renaissance humanist. Shakespeare was also just as interested in individual personality as any of the Italian painters; the only difference was that the Italians used paint and canvas to capture personality, whereas Shakespeare used pen and paper. Finally, one may say that Shakespeare was not only a man of the Renaissance but also a Renaissance man, for he wrote comedies, tragedies, histories, romances, and poems of all sorts. And he excelled at every kind of writing he attempted.

Many of Shakespeare's works were first performed at the Globe Theater (left). The first collected edition of his plays was printed in 1623 (right).

The Renaissance in Spain

The Renaissance also came to Spain relatively late. Spain's greatest Renaissance painter actually was a Greek, born on the isle of Crete and trained in Venice. His name was Domenikos Theotokopoulos (doh MEN ih kohs tha oh toh KOH poo lohs), but after he moved to Spain, in about 1577, he became known as El Greco, which is Spanish for "the Greek."

El Greco spent about 12 years in Venice. There, he learned to paint in the Italian Renaissance manner. He clearly was influenced by the paintings of Titian, as the rich colors of his own paintings bear witness.

From Venice, El Greco traveled to Rome, where his outspokenness did not win him many friends. El Greco learned a lot from artists in Rome, including Michelangelo. But he offended people by criticizing Michelangelo's paintings. When El Greco saw that he had worn out his welcome in Rome, he moved on to the Spanish city of Toledo (tuh LAID oh). El Greco spent the rest of his life in Spain. He received many commissions, often for paintings to adorn churches and chapels. Among his most famous works is a painting known as *The Burial of the Count of Orgaz*. The painting displays the long, slender figures that came to distinguish El Greco's work.

A Great Writer

Renaissance Spain also produced one of the greatest writers of that age, or any age. He was Miguel de Cervantes (mee GEL de sur VAN teez), and his best-known work is the novel *The History of Don Quixote de la Mancha* (dahn kee HOHT ay de la MAHN chah). The hero, Don Quixote, has a noble heart, but he does many foolish things as he tries to imitate the brave knights he has read about. Don Quixote insists that a simple peasant girl he loves is really a noble duchess. He jousts against windmills, thinking they are evil giants. Today, we use the word *quixotic* (kwihks AHT ihk) to describe someone who is impractical or who is striving for an unreachable ideal.

The phrase "tilting at windmills," describing a noble but impractical plan, comes from this scene from Don Quixote.

European Renaissance

As we have seen, the Renaissance began in Italy. It was in Italy that the following characteristics of the period first developed: an enthusiasm for the classical past as a source of inspiration, an interest in accurately portraying the natural world, a fascination with the individual, and an appreciation for artists and their work.

From the Italian city-states of Florence, Venice, and Rome, the spirit and ideals of the Renaissance spread to other countries. But far from simply imitating what had been done in Italy, artists and scholars in other countries developed their own individual styles. What had been done in Italy inspired them to enrich their own local and national traditions. Western civilization has reaped the rewards of their work.

apothecary a druggist or pharmacist

apprentice in the Middle Ages and the Renaissance, someone who agreed to live with and work for another for a specified period, in return for instruction in a trade or craft

basilica a Christian church building, often in the shape of a cross

chateau a French castle, or large country house; *chateaux* is the plural form

diplomat one who represents a government in its relationships with other governments

fresco a painting made on fresh, moist plaster with color pigments dissolved in water

galley a large, flat-bottomed ship propelled by sails and oars and used in the Mediterranean for trade and war

infallible incapable of error; certain

lagoon a shallow body of water, especially one separated from a larger body of water by a sandbar or reef

mason a person who builds or works with brick or stone

patron a wealthy person who supports an artist

perspective a technique that allows artists to show objects as they appear at various distances from the viewer, with distant objects shown smaller and nearby objects larger

prior the person, or officer, in charge of a priory, or monastery

quarry to obtain stone from a pit or excavation by cutting, digging, or blasting it

Renaissance man one who is highly skilled and has broad interests in many or all of the arts and sciences

republic a system of government in which voters elect officials to run the government and make laws

rhetoric the art of using words effectively in speaking or writing

CREDITS

Cover Design: Senja Lauderdale
Interior Design: Denise Ingrassia
Project Editor: Ruth Dittmann